Let's Discover The States

Upper Atlantic

NEW JERSEY • NEW YORK

By
Thomas G. Aylesworth
Virginia L. Aylesworth

CHELSEA HOUSE PUBLISHERS
New York   New Haven   Philadelphia

Created and produced by Blackbirch Graphics, Inc.

DESIGN: Richard S. Glassman
PROJECT EDITOR: Bruce S. Glassman
ASSOCIATE EDITOR: Robin Langley Sommer

Printed in Hong Kong

ISBN: 1-55546-553-6

Summary: Discusses the geographical, historical, and cultural aspects of New Jersey, New York

Uses maps, illustrated fact spreads, and other illustrated materials to highlight subjects of land, history, and
people of each state. Full-color throughout.
Bibliographies
Includes Index.

CONTENTS

cop·1

NEW YORK 29

The tall, slim tower of the Barnegat Lighthouse.
The mountains dotted with skiers, the coastal
  plains visited by vacationers.
Grazing horses and fertile truck farms.
Oil refineries, scientific research centers, and the
  beautiful campus of Princeton University.
The seashore, the forests, and the Delaware River.

Let's Discover

New

Jersey

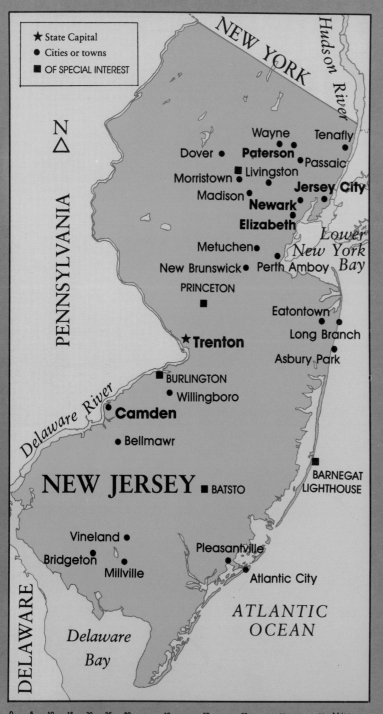

Map Legend:
- ★ State Capital
- ● Cities or towns
- ■ OF SPECIAL INTEREST

△ N

NEW YORK

Hudson River

PENNSYLVANIA

Wayne
Tenafly
Dover ●
Paterson
Passaic
Morristown ● ■ Livingston
Madison ● **Jersey City**
Newark
Elizabeth
Metuchen ●
New Brunswick ● Perth Amboy
Lower New York Bay
PRINCETON ■
Eatontown
★ **Trenton**
Long Branch
Asbury Park

Delaware River

BURLINGTON ■
● Willingboro
Camden
● Bellmawr

NEW JERSEY ■ BATSTO

■ BARNEGAT LIGHTHOUSE

Vineland ●
Bridgeton ●
Pleasantville ●
Millville ●
Atlantic City ●

ATLANTIC OCEAN

DELAWARE

Delaware Bay

| 0 | 5 | 10 | 15 | 20 | 25 | 30 | 40 | 50 | 60 | 70 | 80 Miles |
| 0 | 5 | 10 | 15 | 20 | 25 | 30 | 40 | 50 | 60 | 70 | 80 | 90 | 100 | 110 | 120 | 130 Kilometres |

Capital: Trenton

State Flag

NEW JERSEY
At a Glance

Major Industries: Manufacturing, chemicals, petroleum
Major Crops: Hay, corn, soybeans, truck crops

State Flower: Violet
State Bird: Eastern Goldfinch

Size: 7,787 square miles (46th largest)
Population: 7,515,000 (9th largest)
State Motto: Liberty and Prosperity
State Tree: Red Oak
Nickname: The Garden State

One of the many New Jersey historic districts that has undergone recent restoration.

Dairy farms are a common sight in the Delaware Water Gap region.

The Land

New Jersey is often thought of as a state filled with factories, oil refineries, research laboratories, and industrial towns. But those things are confined mainly to a 15-mile-wide corridor that stretches westward from Newark to Camden on the border. The rest of the state is filled with natural beauty. There are 200-year-old towns with tree-shaded streets. There are more than 800 lakes and ponds, 100 rivers and creeks, and 1400 miles of streams. Add to that 127 miles of beaches stretching from Sandy Hook in northern New Jersey to Cape May in the south. New Jersey as a whole is a state of great variety.

A general store built around the time of the Revolution.

Most of New Jersey is surrounded by water. Its more than 127 miles of beaches are among the most popular in the region.

Except for a 48-mile land border with New York in the north, New Jersey is surrounded by water. The Hudson River and the Atlantic Ocean are on the east. Delaware Bay is on the southwest. And the Delaware River is on the west. Most of the state's soil, except for the salt marshes and sandy areas along the Atlantic Coast, is ideal for farming.

New Jersey has four main land regions. In the northeast is the Appalachian Ridge and Valley Region, part of a mountainous area that runs from New York to Alabama. High Point, the state's highest peak, rises 1,803 feet here. It is part of the Kittatinny Mountains, New Jersey's chief mountain range. The Delaware Water Gap, formed where the Delaware River cuts through the mountains, is located in this region; it is one of the most beautiful areas in the East. Apples and vegetables are the main crops in this part of the state, and herds of dairy cattle graze on the picturesque grassy slopes of the valleys.

The New England Upland, sometimes called the Highlands, is southeast of the Appalachian Ridge and Valley Region. Much of this area is covered with flat-topped ridges of hard rock. But the Highlands are also filled with lovely lakes, which attract sportsmen from all over for fishing, boating, and swimming.

Most of the soil in the state is ideal for farming. Here farmers work at cultivating a bean crop.

Farmers working in a cranberry field in Burlington City. In order to harvest cranberries, the fields in which they grow are filled with water. Once the fields are flooded, the cranberries float to the surface and are easily harvested.

Above:

The Atlantic Coastal Plain is characterized by long, flat lowland and is most prevalent in the southern half of the state.

At right:

Atlantic City, located on the southern coast, is one of the busiest resort towns in the Northeast. Hotels and casinos are among the most popular features of Atlantic City, the only area in the country besides Nevada where organized gambling is legal.

Below:

A beach in Atlantic City near the famous Boardwalk.

The Piedmont crosses the top half of New Jersey northeast to southwest. It is only about 20 miles wide and covers some 20 percent of the state. But almost 75 percent of the people in the Garden State live here. Most of them are in industrial cities like Elizabeth, Jersey City, and Paterson. The reason for this concentration of industry is that so many of the state's rivers are found here, and in the early days before the railroads, goods and manufactured items had to be carried by boat. Among these rivers are the Hudson, the Musconetcong, the Passaic, the Ramapo, and the Raritan.

The rest of the state, south of the Piedmont, is called the Atlantic Coastal Plain. In most places this gently rolling lowland is less than 100 feet above sea level. Truck farms, those farms on which vegetables are grown for the markets, work the fertile soil of the west and southwest parts of this area. At the western edge of the plain are Camden, Trenton, and other cities that lie along the wide Delaware River. In the eastern portion of the Atlantic Coastal Plain there are forests and salt marshes. Since the soil here is rather poor, large portions of this area are thinly populated. But the Atlantic coast has more than 50 resort cities and towns such as Atlantic City, Asbury Park, and Cape May.

A long, narrow sandbar runs along most of the state's 130-mile Atlantic coastline. There are many inlets through this sandbar, which have formed bays between the bar and the mainland. From north to south, the bays are Newark Bay, Raritan Bay, Sandy Hook Bay, Barnegat Bay, Little Egg Harbor, Great Bay, and Great Egg Bay. The coastal regions of New Jersey are among the most popular vacation areas in the United States.

Because of the ocean breezes, the eastern coast of the state has a mild climate—cool in summer and warm in winter. The average January temperatures range from 34 degrees F. in the south to 26 degrees F. in the northwest. Average July temperatures range from 76 degrees F. in the southwest to 70 degrees F. in the north. However, because of its long coastline, New Jersey is susceptible to violent storms sweeping in from the Atlantic Ocean.

Many farms in southern New Jersey grow vegetables that provide the markets in the region with fresh produce.

A "false face" mask, made by one of the tribes of the Iroquois, the Indian nation that ranged across the eastern United States.

The History

There were probably about 8,000 Indians living in what is now New Jersey before the European settlers arrived. They were peaceful Native Americans who called themselves Leni-Lenape—"The Original People." They spent most of their time hunting, but they also raised maize (or corn), beans, squash, and other crops. When white settlers came, they called these Indians of the Algonkian family the Delawares, after their home valley.

Probably the first European to explore the New Jersey coast was Giovanni da Verrazano, an Italian navigator in the service of France, who reached the area in 1524. In 1609 Henry Hudson, an English sea captain employed by the Dutch, explored the area around Sandy Hook Bay and sailed up the river that bears his name. Cornelius Mey, a Dutch explorer, sailed the Delaware River in 1614—Cape May was later named for him. Mey was the founder of Fort Nassau, near the site of today's Glouster City. By 1618 the Dutch had established a trading post at Bergen, and about 1630 they set up another outpost at Pavonia, which is now a part of Jersey City. There were also small Swedish settlements on the Delaware and Maurice Rivers. Still, the Indians had the land pretty much to themselves.

Because they feared Swedish competition in the fur trade, the Dutch forced the Swedes out of New Jersey in 1655. The first permanent settlement in New Jersey was probably that of Bergen, a fortified town that is now also a part of Jersey City.

Then came a change of power. In 1644 Charles II of England granted his brother James, the Duke of York, extensive New World holdings, including what later became known as New Jersey. James, in turn, gave the land to two of his friends, Lord John Berkeley and Sir George Carteret. The Dutch gave up their claim to the area without a fight, and the two Englishmen sold the land to settlers at low prices. One important decision made by Berkeley and Carteret was to allow religious and political freedom in their territory. It was a daring idea for the time, but welcome news to oppressed minorities. Soon people were arriving in droves.

Carteret had been something of a hero in the defense of the Isle of Jersey, one of the English Channel islands off the northwest coast of France. Thus it was he who named the new territory New Jersey.

English colonization progressed rapidly, as Calvinists, Congregationalists, and Presbyterians moved in to civilize the eastern half of the area. In 1674 a group of Quakers, headed by Edward Billynge, bought Berkeley's holdings in the western half of the territory. Two years later, in 1676, the colony was divided into two sections—West Jersey and East Jersey.

When Queen Anne came to the English throne in 1702, she demanded that all the proprietors surrender their rights of government to England. The halves of New Jersey were united into a single royal province. Still, from 1703 to 1775, the colony had two capitals. They were Perth Amboy, the former capital of East Jersey, and Burlington, the former capital of West Jersey. At first, the governor of New York also ruled New Jersey. But the settlers protested, and in 1738 England gave New Jersey its own governor, Lewis Morris.

A monument to the soldiers who died in the Battle of Princeton, 1777. Though the American troops lost one of their finest leaders, General William Mercer, in the fight, their stunning victory over the British under the leadership of General George Washington was an important triumph in the Revolutionary War.

During the Revolutionary War few American troops had a formal uniform. At Skylands, in Jockey Hollow, a modern-day "militiaman" demonstrates the informal dress of most colonial soldiers.

Aaron Burr and former U.S. Secretary of the Treasury Alexander Hamilton were long-time rivals. After a number of fierce political disputes, the two men decided to undertake a duel to the death. Burr, shown here in an engraving by Enoch G. Gridley, was the victor.

By the 1760s the colony had about 100,000 people, and there were rumblings of the coming Revolution. England had imposed severe taxes and restricted the trade of the colony, and the people were becoming discontented. The first Provincial Congress assembled in New Brunswick in 1774 and appointed delegates to the Continental Congress at Philadelphia. On July 2, 1776, the last royal governor of New Jersey was expelled, and the leaders of New Jersey adopted a combined state constitution and declaration of independence. As far as New Jersey was concerned, the Revolution was on.

From that time until the surrender of Lord Cornwallis at Yorktown in 1781, New Jersey knew no peace. The state became known as "the pathway of the Revolution," as the Americans and the British fought nearly 100 engagements on its soil. The most important of these battles were Trenton in 1776, Princeton in 1777, and Monmouth in 1778. Before the Battle of Trenton, George Washington made his famous surprise crossing of the Delaware River on Christmas night, and captured a garrison of Hessian mercenary troops who were in the employ of the British. Washington and his army crossed and recrossed New Jersey four times, shivering through two winters at Morristown and a third at Bound Brook. Tories—colonists loyal to the English Crown—took control of the southern Pine Barrens and waged guerrilla war from there. During the Revolutionary War, two New Jersey cities served temporarily as the national capital: Princeton, from June 30 to November 4, 1783, and Trenton, from November 1 to December 24, 1784.

New Jersey was the third state to ratify the Constitution, in 1787. William Livingston was appointed the first governor, and the state capital was established at Trenton in 1790. One of the most famous duels of all time was fought at Weehawken in 1804, when Aaron Burr, Vice-President of the United States, shot and killed his political rival, Alexander Hamilton. During the War of 1812, in which the United States again fought the British, it was a New Jersey man, Captain James Lawrence, who gave the United States Navy its motto: "Don't give up the ship!"

This engraving, completed two years after the famous Hamilton/Burr duel, depicts the exact spot in Weehawken where Hamilton fell.

During the early 1800s, New Jersey made major improvements in its transportation system, including new turnpikes, canals, and railroads. Better transportation in the state was important to the industrial growth that has continued to the present day.

In 1884 New Jersey became much more democratic when it adopted a new state constitution, which provided for a bill of rights and direct election of the governor by the people. The following year Charles C. Stratton became the first New Jersey governor elected by popular vote.

During the Civil War (1861–65), New Jersey seemed to be of two minds about the conflict. Some 88,000 men from the state served in the Union Army during the war, but many New Jersey residents were pro-South. Indeed, New Jersey was one of only three states in the Union that did not support the re-election of President Abraham Lincoln in 1864.

During the late 1800s, New Jersey, unlike most other states, allowed the formation of trusts, or business and industrial monopolies. This meant that many of the nation's powerful trusts made the state

The home of inventor Thomas A. Edison in West Orange, New Jersey.

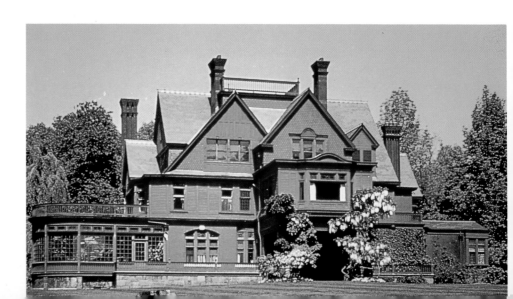

Thomas A. Edison (center) and several of his close assistants pose with an early phonograph outside their laboratory in West Orange, New Jersey, 1888. Edison called his West Orange laboratory the "invention factory."

their home. The same thing was true for holding companies—firms that owned or controlled the stocks and policies of other companies. By the turn of the century, hundreds of these companies had been licensed to set up headquarters in New Jersey, which gave a big boost to the state's economy.

Industrial development was on the rise, too. New Jersey factories were busy turning out elevators, sewing machines, steam locomotives, and other up-to-the-minute products. The farming and food-processing industries expanded, also, as did the iron and steel factories. As a result, the population of New Jersey increased in the early years of the twentieth century. Thousands of immigrants began coming to the cities to work in factories: by 1910 about half the population of the Garden State had either been born outside the United States or had parents who had come from other countries. For the first time, more people lived in New Jersey cities than on New Jersey farms.

In 1910 New Jersey elected as governor the progressive Woodrow Wilson, a former president of Princeton University, and state government began to change for the better. Laws were passed to provide direct primary elections, workman's compensation for job-related injuries or illness, and a public-utilities commission. Business monopolies were restricted. This forward-looking change in state government led to Wilson's election as President of the United States in 1912 and his re-election in 1916. He was a staunch advocate of world peace, who wore out his health seeking support for the League of Nations after World War I.

Fort Lee became the motion picture capital of the world in the early 1900s because of the pioneering film work being done in New Jersey by Thomas Alva Edison. Early stars such as Mary Pickford, Fatty Arbuckle, and Pearl White made many films in the state, which served as a "Wild West" location before the movie industry moved to Hollywood, California.

During World War I, Hoboken was a major port, and thousands of American servicemen left for France from that city on the Hudson River. Camp Dix and Camp Merrit were set up as huge military training centers, and New Jersey factories turned out vast quantities of chemicals, munitions, and ships to aid the war effort.

The years from 1900 to 1930 were years of expansion for the state. The population nearly doubled, and the value of products manufactured in New Jersey grew from $500 million to $4 billion. The state moved into its role as an electronics and chemical giant in the 1940s. New Jersey was a leader in the production of communications equipment, munitions, ships, and uniforms during World War II. Huge numbers of servicemen were trained at Camp Kilmer and Fort Dix.

During the 1950s, New Jersey's transportation system was expanded by construction of both the New Jersey Turnpike, which crosses the state diagonally from southwest to northeast, and the Garden State Parkway, which runs the length of New Jersey's east coast.

Today New Jersey is a state of large cities and small farms, with a wealth of scenic beauty and recreational facilities. New Jersey's cities contain vast industrial complexes, and its farms earn a larger gross income per acre than those of any other state.

A portrait by Eastman Johnson of Stephen Grover Cleveland, twenty-second President of the United States. President Cleveland was the only president ever to be married in the White House. A bachelor when he was elected, he married Frances Folsom on June 2, 1886, in a ceremony that took place in the presidential mansion.

The People

According to the 1984 census, there were 7,515,000 people in New Jersey, 90 percent of whom lived in cities and towns. This percentage of city dwellers is the highest in the nation. About 90 percent of New Jersey's residents were born in the United States. Of those born in other countries, the largest number came from Italy. Roman Catholics make up the state's largest religious body.

A Woodrow Wilson campaign poster from 1910. During his term in office as Governor of New Jersey, Wilson began many of his progressive programs aimed at, among other things, protecting the rights of individuals.

FOR GOVERNOR

WOODROW WILSON

Many New Jerseyites have been prominent in American history and culture. In the field of politics, in addition to Aaron Burr and Woodrow Wilson, there is Grover Cleveland, the 22nd and 24th President of the United States (he served two terms—1885–89 and 1893–97, with Benjamin Harrison serving in between). Cleveland was born in Caldwell, New Jersey.

In the arts, Burlington, New Jersey, can lay claim to James Fenimore Cooper, the early American novelist most famous for *The Last of the Mohicans* from the *Leatherstocking Tales*. Joyce Kilmer, the soldier poet who was killed in World War I, was born in New Brunswick, New Jersey; his best-known poem is 'Trees.' Stephen Crane, the author of the monumental Civil War novel *The Red Badge of Courage,* was born in Newark. The great poet Walt Whitman, and the patriotic pamphleteer Thomas Paine, were New Jersey natives. Pianist and band leader Count Basie came from Red Bank, New Jersey, and one of the nation's finest classical singers and actors, Paul Robeson, was born in Princeton.

Thomas A. Edison was not the only scientist or technologist to call New Jersey his home. Astronaut Walter M. Schirra, Jr., who flew the Mercury-Atlas 8 mission, came from the Garden State, and the great physicist and mathematician Albert Einstein spent many years at Princeton University after emigrating to America from his native Germany. American folk heroine Molly Pitcher was a New Jerseyite, as were military men General George McClellan and Admirals William F. "Bull" Halsey, Jr., and James A. Van Fleet.

In the field of entertainment there are many prominent New Jersey natives. Actors Danny De Vito and Jack Nicholson were both born in Neptune. Other actors from the Garden State are Robert Blake (Nutley), Michael Douglas (New Brunswick), Jerry Lewis (Newark), Roy Scheider (Orange), Meryl Streep (Summit), Loretta Swit (Passaic), and John Travolta (Englewood). Count Basie and Paul Robeson were not the only prominent musicians from New Jersey. Others on the list are Frank Sinatra (Hoboken), Bette Midler (Paterson), and Bruce "The Boss" Springsteen (Freehold).

The New Jersey Nets basketball team hosts its opponents at the Brendan Byrne Arena, named for a former governor of the state.

OF SPECIAL INTEREST

IN PRINCETON: *Princeton University*
Founded in 1746, Princeton is the fourth oldest college in the United States. Nassau
    Hall, built in 1756, served for a time as the meeting place for Congress.

IN BATSTO: *Batsto State Historic Site*
This restored early-nineteenth-century iron and glassmaking community features
    houses, stores, and a blacksmith's shop.

IN BURLINGTON: *The James Fenimore Cooper House*
Built in 1780, this was the home of the famous novelist of pioneer days. Nearby is
    the Captain James Lawrence House, birthplace of the commander of the *Chesa-*
    peake during the War of 1812—the man who cried "Don't give up the ship!"

IN MORRISTOWN: *Morristown National Historical Park*
It was here that the Continental Army wintered in 1779–80, in the fourth year of
    the Revolutionary War. On the grounds are the Ford Mansion (1774), Fort
    Nonsense (1777), and Wick House, which was used by General St. Clair in
    1779–80. Nearby is Jockey Hollow—the Continental Army's headquarters that
    winter.

Visitors at Jockey Hollow can see re-enactments of engagements from the Revolutionary War.

For more information write:
THE STATE DIVISION OF TRAVEL AND TOURISM
CN-384
TRENTON, NEW JERSEY 08625

FURTHER READING

Bill, Alfred H. *New Jersey and the Revolutionary War.* Rutgers University Press,
    1964.
Carpenter, Allan. *New Jersey,* rev. ed. Childrens Press, 1979.
Fleming, Thomas J. *New Jersey: A Bicentennial History.* Norton, 1977.
Fradin, Dennis B. *New Jersey in Words and Pictures.* Childrens Press, 1980.
Resnick, Abraham. *New Jersey: Its People and Culture.* Denison, 1974.
Robertson, Keith. *New Jersey.* Coward, 1969.

The soaring twin towers of the World Trade Center.
"The Long Gray Line" of West Point cadets.
The shrine of our national pastime—the Baseball
  Museum and Hall of Fame.
The mansions of the rich and famous along the
  mighty Hudson River.
The thunderous roar of majestic Niagara Falls.

NEW YORK

At a Glance

Capital: Albany

Major Industries: Communications, finance, timber, minerals, fishing, wine, fruits, vegetables, dairy products

State Flag

State Flower: Rose
Nickname: The Empire State

State Bird: Bluebird

Size: 49,576 square miles (30th largest)
Population: 17,735,000 (2nd largest)

N

VERMONT

MASSACHUSETTS

CONNECTICUT

Long Island Sound

Montauk Point, on the tip of Long Island.

Along the banks of the Hudson River.

Although much of the Adirondack range is mountainous, it does contain areas that are suitable for farming.

The Land

New York is the only state with borders on the Atlantic Ocean and the Great Lakes. It has a 127-mile Atlantic coastline and 371 miles of shoreline on Lake Ontario and Lake Erie. Its tallest mountains are in the Adirondack range, in the northeastern part of the state, and the highest point in these mountains is Mount Marcy, at 5,344 feet. Waterways are important to the state's transportation system. The Hudson and the Mohawk are the chief rivers, followed by the Genesee and the Oswego. New York also has more than 8,000 lakes.

The Ice Age ended about 10,000 years ago, but during that time huge glaciers covered almost all of what is now New York State. Most of the soil here was deposited by these massive ice formations as they scattered stones, pebbles, and other materials over the surface of the land.

New York has seven major land regions. The Atlantic Coastal Plain takes in Long Island and Staten Island as part of the almost level plain stretching along the Atlantic Coast from Massachusetts to the tip of Florida. Broad sandy beaches can be found on the southern shore of Long Island. Fishing and recreation are an important source of income in this area.

The New England Upland, with its hills and low mountains, forms a narrow strip along the state's eastern edge, running from the south toward the northern border. In this area are the Taconic Mountains and the southern part of the Hudson River Valley.

The many ports of Long Island are home to thousands of pleasure boats and other craft like this one in Greenport.

Much of New York State is still naturally wild. Ausable Chasm is a good example of the heavily wooded, rocky land common to the Adirondack region.

The Hudson-Mohawk Lowland covers most of the remaining Hudson River Valley and the whole of the Mohawk River Valley. This strip west of the New England Upland is from 10 to 30 miles wide. It is the only large break in the Appalachian Mountains, and cuts through highlands that can reach heights of a thousand feet or more. This has made it a major "roadway" for trade since Indian times. The plains in this area support countless farms, orchards, and dairies, and the many waterfalls here serve as a source of hydroelectric power.

The Adirondack Upland is in the northeastern part of New York—a circular area whose mountains are perhaps the oldest in North America. These uplands are wild and beautiful, with their mountains, lakes, streams, and waterfalls. The soil here cannot support much farming, but there are lumber mills and iron ore mines.

Chittenango Falls in central New York State.

This farmland is characteristic of the long, flat tracts found in the Atlantic Coastal Plain.

39

A view of Rochester, one of the biggest cities in western New York.

The Catskill countryside is dotted with many covered bridges like this one.

Along the south bank of the St. Lawrence River lies the St. Lawrence Lowland, bordering the Adirondack Upland to the north. Only about 20 miles wide, this region of rolling hills contains many dairy farms and apple orchards, and the tourist industry is important to the Thousand Islands of the St. Lawrence River.

The Erie-Ontario Lowland lies south of the two Great Lakes for which it is named; part of it was once the bottom of an ancient glacial lake. In other parts of the Lowland, moraines, or glacial deposits, form another region of rolling hills. Southeast of Rochester are many drumlins—oval-shaped hills from 50 to 300 feet high. These, too, were formed by the old glaciers. The region has some of the most productive soil in the state, and there are many fruit and truck farms here, as well as dairy farms and plant nurseries.

The Appalachian Plateau covers most of southern New York State, lying south and west of the Hudson-Mohawk Lowland and south of the Erie-Ontario Lowland. In this area, glaciers and rivers have formed hills and valleys in the Finger Lakes area and mountains in the Catskills. Dairy farms are common in this region, as are vineyards, nurseries, and truck farms. It is a scenic area that is popular with vacationers.

The climate of New York State varies greatly from region to region because of the vast differences in altitude and exposure to bodies of water. The coastal areas have the hottest summers, mildest winters, and least snow. The Adirondack Highlands have the heaviest snows, the coldest winters, and the coolest summers. The average temperatures along the coastal plain are 32 degrees F. in January and 76 degrees F. in July. The Adirondacks average 18 degrees F. in January and 64 degrees F. in July. Precipitation here varies between 32 and 45 inches per year, including melted snow.

Above:
New York is one of the country's leading producers of still and sparkling wine. Large vineyards, like this one in Naples, are common sights in the southern half of the state.

Top left:
A view of Lake Ontario, which borders New York at the northwestern part of the state.

41

The History

A harvest mask made by the Onondaga Indians. The Onondaga are one of the Five Nations of the Iroquois and are native to New York.

Before the arrival of the Europeans, there were two Indian groups in what would become New York State. One group was the Algonkian family, which was subdivided into the Delaware, Mohican, Montauk, Munsee, and Wappinger tribes. The other group was the Iroquois, who made up the Five Nations: the Cayuga, Mohawk, Oneida, Onondaga, and Seneca tribes. The Indians farmed, fished, and hunted.

Giovanni da Verrazano, an Italian who was hired by King Francis I of France to explore northern North America, sailed into New York Bay in 1524, and he may have discovered the Hudson River. But no one established strong territorial claims until Henry Hudson piloted the *Half Moon* up the river that bears his name in 1609. The Dutch, for whom he was sailing, founded trading posts at New Amsterdam and at Fort Nassau, 150 miles north. Hudson was looking for a Northwest Passage to the Orient, but his voyage gave the Netherlands a claim to the territory comprising much of present-day New York. In that same year, the French explorer Samuel de Champlain entered the northern part of New York from Quebec. This gave the French a claim to part of the land.

Having built up a profitable fur trade with the Indians of the Hudson Valley, the Dutch merchants formed the Dutch West India Company in 1621, and the government of the Netherlands gave the company the right to trade in what was then called New Netherland for the next 24 years. In 1624 settlement began in earnest with some 30 families sent by the company to the New World. Some of these families founded Fort Orange, the first permanent white settlement in the colony. The next year a group of Dutch colonists built a fort and laid out a town on Manhattan Island—now the heart of New York City—naming the community New Amsterdam. In 1626 the Dutch governor, Peter Minuit, bought Manhattan from the Indians for goods worth 60 Dutch guilders (about $24).

A depiction by John Simon of Etow Oh Koam, an Iroquois chief. The portrait is entitled "King of the River Nation."

This 1642 engraving shows some of New York's original Dutch settlers in their new homeland. Their settlement was called "New Amsterdam."

During the next few years, several towns were established by the Dutch—Wiltwyck, Rensselaerswyck, Breuckelen, Schenectady, and others. Meanwhile, many English settlers from Connecticut and Massachusetts had moved into Long Island. For a time they cooperated with the Dutch, but King Charles II of England coveted the region, and he gave his brother James, the Duke of York, a charter for the territory of New Netherland. In 1664 a British fleet dropped anchor in the harbor of New Amsterdam, and Peter Stuyvesant, the Dutch governor, surrendered without a fight in a bloodless coup—a sudden takeover. Names changed all over the territory. New Amsterdam became New York, as did New Netherland. Fort Orange became Albany; Wiltwyck became Kingston; Rensselaerswyck became Rensselaer; Breuckelen became Brooklyn.

For some time the colony prospered under English rule. Then the French, who had claimed the Lake Champlain area in the north and named it New France, began to take a real interest in the territory. In 1669 the French explorer Robert Cavelier, Sieur de la Salle, entered the Niagara region. Then, in 1689, war broke out in Europe between England and France, and New York became a battleground—an extension of that war. The French built a fortress at Crown Point on Lake Champlain in 1731. They began a steady harassment from the north, sometimes alone and sometimes with Indian allies. Battles were fought at Crown Point, at Niagara, at Fort Ticonderoga, and in many other places, with the Algonkians helping the French and the Iroquois siding with the English and the Loyalists. But despite the loss of life among settlers in what came to be called the French and Indian Wars, the colony continued to prosper. The warring countries finally signed a peace treaty—the Treaty of Paris—in 1763, and France lost most of her New World holdings.

A modern-day example at Fort Ticonderoga of what soldiers looked like during the Colonial War.

Some traces of the Dutch settlers can still be found today. In Tarrytown, New York, this old church is a well-preserved example of Dutch design and craftsmanship.

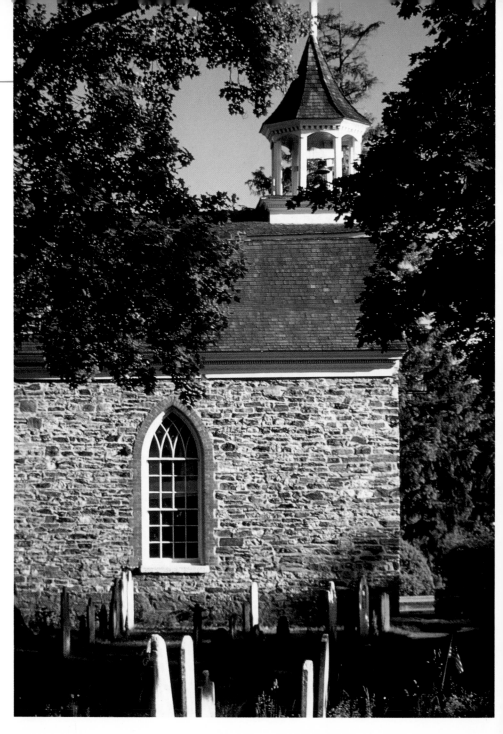

A souvenir from 1850 that shows what New York City looked like at that time.

The British colonists in New York had been granted a Charter of Liberties and Privileges in 1683: it guaranteed a representative assembly with control over taxation, but this began to erode during the reign of King George II. An important victory for freedom of speech and of the press was won in 1735, when the publisher of the *New York Weekly Journal,* John Peter Zenger, who had criticized the English governor, was found not guilty of libel.

It was at Albany in 1754 that the first Colonial Congress adopted a Plan of Union incorporating human-rights principles. This was the initial step toward uniting the 13 original colonies. Many New Yorkers did not like the presence of British troops, the authority of royal judges, or the taxes levied by the British Parliament. Others—the Loyalists or Tories—upheld the British Government and refused to call themselves American patriots.

New York's strategic location made it the place in which a third of the battles of the Revolutionary War were fought—on land and in the water. American patriots won two of the major New York battles. The first was the Battle of Oriskany in August 1777; even more important was the Battle of Saratoga in October 1777, in which British General Burgoyne's defeat turned the tide of the war in the colonists' favor.

On July 9, 1776, the Provincial Congress of New York, meeting in White Plains, approved the Declaration of Independence that the Continental Congress had adopted on July 4. The following year New

York adopted a state constitution with three basic branches of government—legislative, executive, and judicial—12 full years before the Federal Government worked out this form for its own use. George Clinton was installed as the first governor of the state.

When New York ratified the United States Constitution, it became the 11th state to enter the union. No one knows how many New York colonists were loyal to the British cause, but after the Revolution, 30,000 persons left the state. New York City served as the capital of the United States from 1785 to 1790. George Washington was inaugurated the nation's first president in 1789 in New York's Federal Hall.

After the Revolution, settlement of New York State progressed rapidly at the expense of the native peoples. Washington had sent an expedition to subdue the Iroquois in 1779, and troops led by General James Clinton raided Indian villages throughout the Mohawk Valley. These soldiers joined others commanded by General John Sullivan and marched through the Finger Lakes reigon to the Genesee Valley in Pennsylvania. The Iroquois were dispossessed and defeated, and many Revolutionary War veterans moved into the desirable territory.

During the War of 1812, much of the fighting took place in frontier regions near the New York-Canadian border. The joint land-lake victory of General Macomb and Commodore Macdonough at Plattsburg broke the strength of British attacks from the north. After the war, pioneers began to settle in the northern and western sections of the state, and by 1820 New York had reached a population level of over 1,370,000—greater than that of any other state.

New York's long-awaited Erie Canal opened in 1825, under the leadership of Governor DeWitt Clinton, the nephew of George Clinton: it provided low-cost transportation from the Great Lakes to the Atlantic. New industries sprang up from New York City to Buffalo, where the canal began. The development of railroads across the state soon followed.

Long before the beginning of the Civil War in 1861, most New Yorkers opposed slavery, but there were dissenters. In July of 1863

Fraunces Tavern was one of George Washington's favorite meeting places in New York City. The city served as the capital of the United States from 1785 to 1790.

A statue of George Washington stands on Wall Street in Manhattan, near the spot where he was inaugurated the first President of the United States.

The Statue of Liberty, which stands on Liberty Island in New York Harbor, is America's symbol of freedom and opportunity for people of all races and creeds. It was given to the United States by France as a token of friendship.

mobs rioted in New York City for four days in opposition to drafting men into the Union Army. The mobs set fires, looted, and killed or wounded about 1000 people. The riots were finally stopped by troops called in from the battlefields. Despite all this, New York provided more soldiers, supplies and money for the Union war effort than any other state.

After the Civil War, manufacturing increased all over New York, which had already become known as the Empire State. Waves of immigrants poured in to work in the factories, many of them from Italy, Poland, Russia, and other southern and eastern European countries. By 1900 there were more than 7,000,000 people living in the state. It led the nation in industry, finance, culture, and international trade. Millions of immigrants entered the country at New York City's Ellis Island, passing the great Statue of Liberty as they arrived.

Buffalo hosted a Pan American Exposition in 1901—an international fair that sought to promote understanding between North and South America. The governor of New York from 1899 to 1901 was Theodore Roosevelt, who came from a wealthy old family and had been the Commissioner of Police in New York City. He was a reformer, especially in the field of labor. Roosevelt became Vice-President of the United States under William McKinley. On September 6, 1901, just six months after his inauguration, McKinley was shot by an assassin at the opening ceremonies of the Exposition. Roosevelt became president eight days later when McKinley died.

When the United States entered World War I in 1917, New York City served as the main port from which troop ships sailed to and from Europe. During the Depression of the 1930s, Franklin Delano Roosevelt, a former governor of New York and a cousin of Theodore Roosevelt, became president of the United States. He served from 1933 until his death in 1945—the only U.S. President to be elected to a fourth term. His great popularity was a result of his aggressive leadership through the Depression and war years.

Another great World's Fair was held in New York in 1939 and 1940—this time in New York City. It celebrated "The World of

Niagara Falls, located in the westernmost region of New York State, is a natural wonder that has attracted visitors since the early nineteenth century.

Tomorrow" and introduced a working television set to the American public. Then came World War II, from 1941 to 1945, for which New York produced more war materials than any other state. Binghamton, Buffalo, New York City, Schenectady and other industrial cities converted their plants into war goods production centers that supplied the armed forces. New York Harbor was filled with troop ships again, and plane spotters manned the city's roofs.

The year after the war ended, the United Nations chose New York City as its headquarters. The peacekeeping organization moved into its new office complex on the East River in 1952, making New York a true world capital.

The St. Lawrence Seaway was opened in 1959, on the great river between New York State and the Canadian province of Ontario. Now New York's northern river and Great Lakes ports were ocean ports, with access to the Atlantic. Completion of the 559-mile New York State Thruway (later named for former Governor Thomas E. Dewey) made the state an even more important transportation center by 1960. Creation of the vast State University of New York made higher education available to more young men and women, and cooperation with Canada resulted in great hydroelectric projects along the St. Lawrence River and at Niagara Falls. Today the state of New York is one of the most progressive and productive in the nation.

The World Trade Center's twin towers rise high above the Manhattan skyline at the southern tip of the island. They are the second-tallest buildings in the world and are the central structures in the World Trade Center complex.

The United Nations building is located in midtown Manhattan and is a meeting place for leaders and diplomats from countries all over the world.

New York City typifies the
"melting pot," with its varied
mix of people.

The People

About 85 percent of the residents of New York State live in cities.
New York City, with 7,086,096 citizens, is the most populous city in
the country. Both state and city have been called a "melting pot,"
where people of various races and countries have settled and adopted
a common culture. Almost one in every seven people in the state was
born in another country. One fourth of those who were born in the
United States have a parent or parents who were born in another
country. The largest groups of immigrants came from Italy, Germany,
Russia, Poland, Ireland, Canada, Austria, and Great Britain.

The largest single religious body in the state is the Roman Catholic
Church. New York has more Roman Catholics and more Jews than
any other state.

St. Patrick's Cathedral, with its majestic spires and detailed stonework, is an important seat of the Catholic community in New York.

A Hasidic Jew with his child in Brooklyn. New York has the highest Jewish population in the country.

Above:
Sagamore Hill in Oyster Bay, Long Island, N.Y. Teddy Roosevelt lived here with his second wife after they were married in 1886.

Above right:
Theodore Roosevelt, the twenty-sixth President of the United States, is one of New York's most famous natives. Although he was instrumental in acquiring the use of the Panama Canal for the United States, he is better remembered for his dramatic leadership of the U.S. Cavalry in the Spanish-American War. When President William McKinley was assassinated, Roosevelt took the oath of office at the age of 42 years and ten months. He was the youngest person ever to serve as president.

Many famous statesmen have come from New York, including four presidents—Martin Van Buren from Kinderhook, Millard Fillmore from Locke, Theodore Roosevelt from New York City, and Franklin Delano Roosevelt from Hyde Park.

In culture and the arts, New York has been prolific. Henry James, the philosopher; Herman Melville (New York City), the author of *Moby Dick;* the poet William Cullen Bryant; the editor Horace Greeley; Washington Irving (New York City), creator of *The Legend of Sleepy Hollow* and *Rip Van Winkle;* sportswriter and short-story author Damon Runyon; novelist Edith Wharton (New York City)—all lived in New York. So did reformers Susan B. Anthony, Elizabeth Cady Stanton (Johnstown), Margaret Sanger (Corning), and religious leader Frances Cabrini.

In the field of invention, photographic pioneer George Eastman (Waterville), was a New Yorker, as were Glenn H. Curtiss (Hammondsport), one of the fathers of aviation, and Robert Fulton, the inventor of the steamboat.

The home of Franklin Delano Roosevelt in Hyde Park.

A portrait by Henry Salem Hubbell of native New Yorker Franklin Delano Roosevelt, the thirty-second President of the United States. Roosevelt is best known for his "New Deal" programs, which dramatically restructured government and helped America recover from the Great Depression of the 1930s. Roosevelt was the only president to be elected four times. In total, he served in our nation's highest office for 12 years and 39 days.

New York City has long been considered one of the cultural capitals of the world. Lincoln Center in Manhattan, is home to the Metropolitan Opera, the New York City Ballet, the Vivian Beaumont Theater, and Avery Fisher Hall, pictured here.

The mix of cultures in New York is among the broadest in the world. Rockefeller Center celebrates the traditions of many countries and also serves as a major center for the television, radio, and publishing media.

An inside view of the Guggenheim Museum in New York City. The museum contains many works of modern art in an unusual building designed by famous architect Frank Lloyd Wright.

New York State has had more than its share of political leaders, too. In addition to the presidents and Governor Dewey, there have been such people as James A. Farley (Grassy Point), the postmaster general under Franklin D. Roosevelt; associated with New York City are diplomat Averell Harriman, Senator Jacob K. Javits, Mayor Fiorello H. La Guardia, and Governor Alfred E. Smith.

New York has always been a breeding ground for show business personalities. Among the actors born in New York City are M*A*S*H star Alan Alda, Mel Brooks, and George Burns. Brooklyn was the birthplace of Woody Allen, Danny Kaye, Mary Tyler Moore, and Eddie Murphy. Other acting notables are Lucille Ball (Jamestown), Kirk Douglas (Amsterdam), Valerie Harper (Suffern), and Michael Landon (Forest Hills). New Yorkers in the field of popular music are Joan Baez (Staten Island), Pat Benatar (Brooklyn), Sammy Davis, Jr. (Manhattan), and Barbra Streisand (Brooklyn).

Perhaps the most famous show-business site in the country, Broadway offers an enormous choice of concerts, musicals, dramas, and movies in the hundreds of theaters that line its streets. Broadway productions through the years have launched the careers of countless stars of stage and screen.

OF SPECIAL INTEREST

The Brooklyn Bridge with the World Trade Towers in the background.

NEW YORK CITY: *Major attractions include:*
The Statue of Liberty, the Lincoln Center for the Performing Arts, numerous museums (including the renowned Metropolitan Museum), the Broadway theater district, and such architectural wonders as the Empire State Building, the Chrysler Building, the World Trade Center, and the Brooklyn Bridge. With a population of over 16 million, the New York metropolitan area is the largest in America.

IN TARRYTOWN: *Sleepy Hollow Restorations*
Includes Sunnyside, Washington Irving's Hudson River estate; Philipsburg Manor, an early eighteenth-century grist mill and farmsite; and Van Cortland Manor, a Revolutionary-War-era estate.

IN COOPERSTOWN: *National Baseball Museum and Hall of Fame*
The annual Hall of Fame Baseball Game is held here on Doubleday Field, and the museum commemorates the birthplace of the national game.

IN HYDE PARK: *The Franklin D. Roosevelt National Historic Site*
It includes the president's home, grave, and library, which houses his books, ship models, and personal belongings.

IN NIAGARA FALLS: *Niagara Falls*
The most famous waterfall in the world affords a view of 500,000 tons of water per minute plunging into a deep gorge on the Niagara River.

For more information write:
STATE DEPARTMENT OF COMMERCE, DIVISION OF TOURISM
ONE COMMERCE PLAZA
ALBANY, NEW YORK 12245

FURTHER READING

Bliven, Bruce, Jr. *New York: A Bicentennial History.* Norton, 1981.
Carpenter, Allan. *New York,* rev. ed. Childrens Press, 1978.
Ellis, David M. *New York: The Empire State,* 5th ed. Prentice-Hall, 1980.
Pink, William B. *Getting to Know New York State.* Coward, 1971.
Roseberry, Cecil R. *From Niagara to Montauk: The Scenic Pleasures of New York State.* State University of New York Press, 1982.

INDEX

(numbers in italics refer to illustrations)

Photo Credits/Acknowledgments

Photos on pages 5, 6–7, 8–9, 10, 11, 12, 13, 14, 15, 18, 19, 22, 23, 27, 28 courtesy New Jersey Travel & Tourism; pages 16, 42 courtesy Museum of the American Indian; pages 20, 25, 26, 43, 56 (above right), 5 (bottom) courtesy National Portrait Gallery, Smithsonian Institution; pages 21, 44, 47 courtesy New York Public Library/Stokes Collection; pages 29, 33, 34, 35, 36, 37, 38, 39, 40, 41, 45, 46, 49, 50, 52, 53 (left), 55 (left), 56 (left), 57 (top), 58, 60, 61, 62 courtesy New York State Department of Commerce, pages 30–31, 53 (right), 54, 59 Bruce Glassman, page 55 (right) Ira Toff.

Cover photograph courtesy New York State Department of Commerce.

The Publisher would like to thank Debbie Van Buren, Dawn M. Blauth of the New Jersey Travel & Touris Office, and John C. Cusano of the New York State Department of Commerce for their gracious assistance the preparation of this book.